STEP·BY·STEP

SCOTTISH
Cooking

The Family Circle Promise of Success

Welcome to the world of Confident Cooking, created for you in the
Family Circle Test Kitchen, where recipes are double–tested by our team
of home economists to achieve a high standard of success.

MURDOCH BOOKS®
Sydney • London • Vancouver

BASIC SCOTTISH PANTRY

Over many centuries, the Scots have utilised ingredients from the land and sea to create a pleasantly simple yet flavoursome cuisine. Salted and smoked, earthy and game flavours all contribute to its beauty.

Atholl Brose: A celebratory alcoholic beverage made in the Scottish household by steeping fine ground oatmeal in warm water, straining and reserving the infused liquid, which is later sweetened with a subtly flavoured honey. It is poured into large bottles or jars and topped up with the finest whisky. It is left to stand before being used. The slightly sweet, yet nutty, potent balance is popular on occasions such as Burns' Night.

Bannock, Selkirk: Yeast-based sultana loaf or round, often sweet, which dates back to the mid-19th century. Originally, this bannock was cooked on a griddle and served on special occasions. Savoury, unleavened bannocks are also made with oatmeal; they are served at meal times instead of bread/baps.

Cod: For centuries, this has been the fish most readily available in salted form. Cod is usually boiled, poached or baked and is served with either a mustard, parsley or egg sauce. Scots treasure the head of the cod. They cook it seasoned with a preparation of fish, liver and oatmeal.

Fish: Fresh or dried/salted fish are very popular in Scottish cooking. Herrings soaked in brine, then smoke-cured, are known as kippers. Also popular are haddock, whiting and salmon which are briefly wood-smoked.

Game: Includes grouse, pigeon, partridges, goose, turkey, duck, pheasant, venison and rabbit. Game animals are sometimes larded, wrapped with strips of bacon fat to keep them moist during cooking. Game are usually very lean animals.

Grouse: Traditionally hung for several days to develop its flavour before being cooked in a closed vessel on the stove or roasted in the oven and served with bread sauce, gravy and potato crisps. Older, aged birds are best for casseroles, pies and pâtés.

Haggis: This is the national sausage of Scotland, dating back to the ancient Celts. Traditionally a ball-

shaped sausage made using either the sheep's stomach or ox bung for the skin. This skin is then filled with a mixture of chopped heart, lung, liver, suet and oatmeal. Order the ox bung for Haggis from your butcher. Haggis is often served on New Year's Day, St Andrew's Day and Burns' Night, accompanied by whisky, creamed potatoes, mashed turnips and swedes.

Herring: This is almost the national fish of Scotland. It is a favourite that is either fried, grilled, stuffed and/or baked, usually with oatmeal.

Hogmanay: This is the name for Scottish New Year. Both Het Pint (egg nog) and the famous Haggis sausage are often served on this special occasion.

Meat: Best cuts of beef are used for roasts, fillets and steaks and mince. Lamb (mutton) is often used for pie fillings, soups and casseroles. Offal from both animals, including tongue, liver, heart, lungs, kidneys, tripe and sweetbreads, is also appreciated by the Scots.

Oatmeal: Staple ingredient of Scotland (next to potatoes), particularly in the north. It is used in porridge, biscuits, cakes, dumplings, drinks and as a coating or stuffing for fish, meat, poultry. Available fine, medium or coarse ground.

Porridge: Particularly common at the Scottish breakfast table. It is made with either oatmeal or rolled oats and then served with honey, toasted oatmeal, milk and cream. It is sometimes drizzled with whisky for warmth in the colder months.

Skirlie: Often served as an accompaniment to meats, game birds, seafood and potato dishes. It is made by sautéeing chopped onions in suet or lard over very low heat before stirring in fine oatmeal and cooking it until the mixture is thick. Skirlie can also be used as a stuffing for chicken, rolled into balls and steamed, dropped into simmering stock and cooked as dumplings or packed into a pudding basin and steamed.

Place fruit and whisky in a large mixing bowl. Add rinds and stir.

Beat butter and sugar in small mixing bowl. Add eggs gradually. Beat.

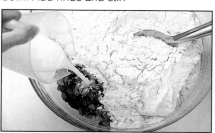

Fold in sifted, dry ingredients. Add ground almonds, milk.

Carefully press blanched almonds in a pattern over surface of cake.

BAKING

In Scotland, baking is a traditional part of most meals, including the hearty breakfast, which often includes soft, warm baps straight from the oven.

Dundee Cake

A famous traditional fruit cake with a rich flavour.

Preparation time:
20 minutes
Total cooking time:
1 hour 15 minutes
+ 20 minutes
standing
Makes 20 cm cake

1¼ cups sultanas
⅔ cup currants
½ cup chopped
raisins
¼ cup chopped peel
2 tablespoons whisky
1 teaspoon grated
lemon rind
1 teaspoon grated
orange rind
150 g butter

⅔ cup (150 g) soft
brown sugar
3 eggs, lightly beaten
1½ cups plain flour
½ teaspoon baking
powder
1 tablespoon ground
almonds
⅓ cup milk
50 g blanched
almonds

---

1 Preheat oven to moderately slow 160°C. Brush a deep round 20 cm cake tin with melted butter or oil. Line base and side with baking paper; grease paper. Place sultanas, currants, raisins, peel, whisky and rinds in a large mixing bowl; stir.

2 Using electric beaters, beat butter and sugar in small mixing bowl until light and creamy. Add eggs gradually, beating thoroughly after each addition. Transfer mixture to large bowl with fruit. 3 Sift flour and baking powder onto fruit and creamed mixture; add ground almonds and milk. Using a metal spoon, fold ingredients together until just combined.

4 Spoon mixture into prepared tin; smooth surface. Press blanched almonds decoratively over surface of cake. Bake 1 hour 15 minutes or until a skewer comes out clean when inserted in centre of cake. Leave cake in tin 20 minutes before inverting onto a wire rack to cool.

Note: This famous rich fruit cake will keep for six to eight weeks in an airtight container. It is suitable for use as a celebration cake for weddings, Christmas or christenings. Decorate according to your special needs.

Black Bun

Make several weeks ahead so it will mature.

Preparation time:
40–50 minutes
Total cooking time:
2½ hours
Makes one 23 cm loaf

2½ cups plain flour
180 g butter, chopped
1 tablespoon caster sugar
2 egg yolks
2 tablespoons iced water
375 g (2½ cups) chopped raisins
300 g (2¼ cups) currants
½ cup dried mixed peel
100 g (½ cup) chopped blanched almonds
⅔ cup caster sugar, extra

1 teaspoon allspice
1 teaspoon ground ginger
1 teaspoon ground cinnamon
2 tablespoons whisky
⅔ cup plain flour
¼ teaspoon cream of tartar
¼ teaspoon bicarbonate of soda
½ cup buttermilk
1 egg plus 1 egg yolk, lightly beaten
1 egg white, lightly beaten
1 teaspoon crystal sugar

---

1 Brush a 23 x 13 x 7 cm non-stick loaf tin with oil. Place flour and butter in food processor; add sugar. Process for 10 seconds or until mixture is fine and crumbly. Add yolks and water, process 15 seconds or until mixture forms a soft dough. Leave, covered with plastic wrap, in refrigerator 20 minutes.

2 Preheat oven to moderate 180°C. Place fruit, peel, almonds, sugar, spices and whisky in large mixing bowl; stir. Sift flour, tartar and soda over fruit; add milk, egg and extra yolk. Using a wooden spoon, beat until well combined.

3 Roll out two-thirds of pastry large enough to cover base and sides of prepared tin, extending 1.5 cm over the top edge. Spoon fruit filling firmly into tin; smooth surface. Roll out the remaining pastry large enough to cover tin. Brush edge of pastry in tin, as well as the fruit filling, with lightly beaten egg white.

4 Place pastry lid over fruit; press to seal. Pinch or flute edges, trimming any excess if necessary. Brush top of black bun with remaining egg white; sprinkle with sugar. Bake 1 hour, then reduce temperature to moderately slow 160°C for a further 1½ hours or until well browned. Cool in tin. Store up to one year.

Add yolks and water and process until mixture forms a soft dough.

Add milk, egg and extra yolk to bowl. Combine using wooden spoon.

Spoon fruit filling firmly into tin. Smooth the surface with a spoon.

After brushing top of black bun with egg white, sprinkle top with sugar.

Scottish Shortbread

Preparation time:
12 minutes
Total cooking time:
35 minutes
Makes 27 cm round

250 g butter	**1/2 cup rice flour**
2/3 cup caster sugar	**1 teaspoon crystal**
12/3 cups plain flour	**sugar**

1 Preheat oven to moderately slow 160°C. Brush a 28 cm round pizza tray with melted butter or oil. Line with baking paper. Using electric beaters, beat butter and sugar in small mixing bowl until light and creamy.
2 Transfer mixture to large mixing bowl; add sifted flours. Using a flat-bladed knife, mix to a soft dough. Transfer mixture onto lightly floured surface. Knead 30 seconds or until smooth.
3 Place dough on prepared tray. Press into a 25 cm round (see Note). Pinch and flute the edge decoratively with your fingers. Prick surface lightly with a fork and mark into 16 segments, using a sharp knife.
4 Sprinkle shortbread with sugar. Bake for 35 minutes on middle shelf until firm and lightly golden. Cool shortbread on tray.
Note: The tray must be larger than the uncooked shortbread round as the mixture will spread during cooking.

HINT
For special occasions decorate the shortbread with almonds or candied orange or lemon peel. Shortbread can also be pressed into a lightly floured shortbread mould. Refrigerate 30 minutes. Turn onto lined baking tray and cook. For extra flavour, add one teaspoon coconut essence or one teaspoon grated orange or lemon rind to butter and sugar in Step 1.

Beat butter and sugar in small mixing bowl until light and creamy.

Using a flat-bladed knife, mix until a soft dough forms.

On prepared tray, press dough with fingers into a 25 cm round.

After marking into segments with a sharp knife, sprinkle shortbread with sugar.

Scottish Oatcakes

Preparation time:
5 minutes
Total cooking time:
25 minutes
Makes 25

1 cup fine oatmeal	*½ teaspoon salt*
1 cup medium oatmeal	*1 teaspoon caster sugar*
½ teaspoon baking powder	*60 g lard, melted*
	½ cup warm water

1 Preheat oven to moderate 180°C. Line two 32 x 28 cm oven trays with baking paper. Combine oatmeals, baking powder, salt and sugar in large mixing bowl. Make a well in centre; add lard and water.
2 Using a flat-bladed knife, mix to a firm dough. Turn onto a surface lightly sprinkled with fine oatmeal; press into a flattish square.
3 Roll dough out to a 30 x 30 cm square (about 3 mm thick), sprinkling with extra oatmeal if necessary. Cut into 6 cm diamonds. Repeat with leftover dough.
4 Place oatcakes on trays about 5 mm apart, bake for 25 minutes. Allow to cool on trays.

Add lard and water to bowl. Mix with a flat-bladed knife to a firm dough.

On a surface lightly sprinkled with fine oatmeal, press dough into a flattish square.

Cut into 6 cm squares or diamonds, using a sharp knife.

Place the prepared oatcakes on trays about 5 mm apart.

Selkirk Bannock

Slice and serve plain or buttered.

Preparation time:
1 hour
40 minutes
Total cooking time:
40 minutes
Makes 28 cm round

---

7 g sachet dried yeast
1 teaspoon caster
  sugar
2 tablespoons plain
  flour
1½ cups lukewarm
  milk

4 cups plain flour,
  extra
1 teaspoon salt
½ cup caster sugar
⅓ cup mixed peel
⅔ cup sultanas
100 g lard or butter,
  melted

---

1 Brush a 28 cm round pizza tray with melted butter. Combine yeast, sugar and flour in medium bowl. Gradually add milk; blend until smooth. Stand, covered with plastic wrap, in warm place 10 minutes or until foamy.

2 Sift extra flour, salt and sugar into large bowl. Add mixed peel and sultanas; stir. Make a well in centre, add yeast mixture and lard. Using a knife, mix to a soft dough.
3 Turn dough onto lightly floured surface, knead for 3 minutes or until smooth. Shape dough into a ball, place in large, lightly oiled bowl. Leave, covered with plastic wrap, in warm place for 1 hour or until well risen.
4 Heat oven to moderately hot 210°C (190°C gas). Knead dough again for 2 minutes or until smooth. Roll dough out large enough to fit prepared tray. Leave, covered with plastic wrap, in warm place for 20 minutes. Make deep random indents into bannock with finger. Bake for 40 minutes until well browned. Stand 5 minutes on tray before transferring to wire rack to cool.

Gradually add milk to bowl. Blend until quite smooth.

Add yeast mixture and lard or butter to bowl. Mix to a soft dough.

On a lightly floured surface, knead dough for 3 minutes.

Make deep random indents into bannock with finger.

Scottish Baps

Serve warm with bacon for a hearty, filling breakfast.

Preparation time:
1 hour 45 minutes
(including proving
and rising)
Total cooking time:
30 minutes
Makes 12

7 g sachet dried yeast	*1½ teaspoons salt*
1 teaspoon caster sugar	*45 g lard or butter, melted*
3½ cups plain flour	*1 tablespoon plain flour, extra*
1 cup lukewarm milk	

1 Lightly dust two 32 x 28 cm oven trays with flour. Combine yeast, sugar and 2 tablespoons flour in bowl. Gradually add milk; blend until smooth. Stand, covered with plastic wrap, in warm place 10 minutes or until foamy. Sift remaining flour and salt in large bowl. Make well in centre, add lard or butter and yeast mix. Using knife, mix to soft dough.

2 Turn dough onto lightly floured surface, knead 3 minutes or until smooth. Shape into ball, place in large, oiled bowl. Leave, covered with plastic, in warm place 1 hour or until well risen.

3 Heat oven to moderately hot 210°C (190°C gas). Knead dough again for 2 minutes or until smooth. Divide into 12 pieces. Knead one portion at a time on lightly floured surface for 1 minute, roll into ball, shape into flat oval. Repeat with remaining dough.

4 Place ovals onto prepared trays; dust with extra flour. Leave, covered with plastic wrap, in warm place 15 minutes or until well risen. Make an indent in centre of each oval with finger. Bake 30 minutes until well browned and cooked through. Cool.

Stand, covered with plastic wrap, in a warm place.

Shape dough into a ball. Place in lightly oiled bowl.

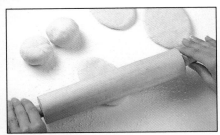

Roll each piece into a ball. Shape into a flat oval.

With finger, make an indent in centre of each oval.

After trimming meat of excess fat and sinew, cut into 5 mm cubes.

Place a portion of filling onto centre of pastry. Brush pastry with water.

SNACKS

Scottish snacks are often quite heavy and filling, to compensate for the harsh climate and lifestyle. Some of these dishes would make a satisfying lunch.

Forfar Bridies

Also served for lunch.

Preparation time:
25 minutes
Total cooking time:
1 hour 20 minutes
Makes 6

750 g boneless sirloin steak	*1/3 cup prepared/ packaged suet mix*
salt, pepper	*1/4 cup rich beef stock*
1 teaspoon dry mustard powder	*2 x 285 g packets flaky pastry mix*
1 large onion, grated	

1 Preheat oven to moderately hot 210°C (190°C gas). Brush a 30 x 28 cm oven tray with oil. Trim meat of excess fat and sinew. Cut into 5 mm cubes; place in a medium bowl. Add salt and pepper, mustard, onion, suet and stock; mix well.

2 Prepare pastry following directions on packet. Divide pastry and meat mixture into six portions. Roll one portion of pastry at a time into a circle 17 cm in diameter.

3 Place a portion of meat filling onto centre of round. Brush outer edge of half the circle with water. Bring pastry over filling to form a half moon. Pinch or flute pastry edge. Stand upright on prepared tray. Repeat with remaining pastry and filling.

4 Bake 20 minutes. Reduce temperature to moderate 180°C and bake further 1 hour or until firm and lightly browned.

Form pastry into half moon shape. Pinch or flute edge.

Bake until bridies are firm and lightly browned.

Scotch Woodcock

Serve freshly made.

Preparation time:
15 minutes
Total cooking time: ·
25 minutes
Serves 4

4 slices bread, crusts removed	60 g butter, softened
45 g can anchovy fillets in oil, drained	3 eggs, lightly beaten
	½ cup cream
2 teaspoons lemon juice	1 tablespoon finely chopped fresh parsley
	pinch cayenne pepper

1 Preheat oven to moderate 180°C. Cut bread diagonally in half. Arrange the triangles on an ungreased 30 x 28 cm oven tray. Bake in oven for 20 minutes or until crisp and golden. Remove from oven; cool on tray.
2 Place anchovies and juice in a small bowl. Mash with a fork to form a paste. Gradually blend in all but 1 teaspoon butter; stir until smooth.
3 Spread one side of toasted triangles with the anchovy butter mixture. Arrange two triangles on each serving plate.
4 Place eggs, cream, parsley and cayenne pepper in medium mixing bowl. Whisk until well combined. Heat remaining butter in small pan, add egg mixture. Stir with a wooden spoon over low heat for 4 minutes or until just cooked. Remove from heat. Spoon mixture over the anchovy toasts.

HINT
The egg mixture for this dish may also be cooked over boiling water in a double boiler for a smoother, creamier texture. This will take longer than the 4 minutes specified in this recipe. Cook the eggs just before serving. If the strong, salty taste of anchovies does not appeal, sardines may be substituted.

Arrange triangles of bread on ungreased oven tray.

Gradually blend in all but 1 teaspoon of butter, stir until smooth.

Spread one side of toasted triangles with anchovy butter.

Stir with a wooden spoon over low heat until just cooked.

Scotch Eggs

Take on a picnic.

Preparation time:
15 minutes
Total cooking time:
8 minutes
Makes 4

---

250 g *sausage mince*
1 *small onion, grated*
2 *tablespoons dried*
  breadcrumbs
1 *egg, separated*
1 *tablespoon chopped*
  fresh parsley

salt, pepper
pinch nutmeg
4 *hard-boiled eggs*
1/2 *cup dried*
  breadcrumbs, extra
oil for deep-frying

1 Place mince, onion, breadcrumbs, egg yolk, parsley, salt, pepper and nutmeg in bowl. Stir to combine.

2 Divide mixture into four. Using wet hands, press one portion of mince large enough to cover egg, into palm of hand. Press mixture over egg to enclose. Repeat with remaining mince and eggs.

3 Coat scotch eggs in lightly beaten egg white, coat with breadcrumbs.

4 Heat oil in heavy-based pan. Lower eggs into oil, cook over medium heat 8 minutes until golden and crisp. Remove from oil. Drain.

Combine mince, onion, breadcrumbs, yolk, parsley, salt, pepper and nutmeg in bowl.

Press portion of mixture around each hard-boiled egg, enclosing the egg.

Brush scotch eggs with lightly beaten egg white and coat with breadcrumbs.

Carefully remove from oil with slotted spoon. Drain on paper towel.

Scottish Crumpets

Preparation time:
8 minutes
Total cooking time:
16 minutes
Makes 9

3/4 cup self-raising
flour
1 tablespoon caster
sugar
1/4 teaspoon baking
powder

1 egg, lightly beaten
2/3 cup milk
10 g butter, melted

---

1 Sift flour, sugar and baking powder in medium mixing bowl.
2 Make a well in centre, gradually add egg and milk. Beat until ingredients are well combined and mixture is smooth.
3 Brush a flat, non-stick pan and five egg rings with the butter. Place egg rings evenly apart in pan.

Heat pan on low 1 minute.
4 Place two tablespoons of mixture into each egg ring. Cook over very low heat for 8 minutes without turning. Crumpets are cooked when the surface has set and bubbles stop rising to the surface. Repeat with the remaining mixture.

Note: It is best to re-grease egg rings each time before use. Lift crumpet and ring together out of the pan. Run a sharp knife around edge to release crumpet from ring. Also known as Scots Crumpets and Tea Pancakes.

HINT

To make an even lighter crumpet, separate the eggs, beat whites until stiff and add them to the mixture last. Crumpets are best eaten warm from the pan, or toasted. They are delicious served plain with butter or with your favourite sweet or savoury topping. Try jam or honey or savoury ham and cheese.

Sift flour, sugar and baking powder into medium mixing bowl.

Make a well in centre, gradually add egg and milk.

Brush five egg rings with butter and place evenly apart in pan.

Place two tablespoons of mixture into each egg ring.

Drop Scones

Similar to pikelets.

Preparation time:
  10 minutes
Total cooking time:
  12 minutes
Makes 40

1 cup self-raising flour	*¼ teaspoon salt*
1 tablespoon caster sugar	*2 eggs, lightly beaten*
	½ cup milk
	25 g butter, melted

1 Sift flour, sugar and salt in medium mixing bowl. Make a well in centre. Add combined eggs, milk and butter.
2 Using a wooden spoon, gradually work the liquid into the dry ingredients to form a smooth batter; do not overbeat.
3 Heat a large, flat non-stick frying pan over low heat for 5 minutes. Drop two teaspoons of mixture onto base of pan about 2 cm apart.
4 Cook over low heat 2 minutes or until top is bubbly and underside is golden. Turn scones over and cook other side 30 seconds. Remove from pan; repeat process with remaining mixture.
Note: To make larger scones, cook a tablespoon of mixture at a time.

Add combined eggs, milk and butter to sifted dry ingredients.

Work liquid in to form a smooth batter. Do not overbeat.

Drop two teaspoons of mixture onto base of pan about 2 cm apart.

When top is bubbly and underside is golden, turn scones over.

After soaking dried peas overnight, rinse and drain well.

Place peas, barley, chops and water in a large pan and bring to boil.

SOUPS, STARTERS & ACCOMPANIMENTS

These wholesome soups are also suitable as a main course. Serve with warm buttered baps followed by a selection of cakes.

Scotch Broth

A one-pot, hearty, filling soup, for cold winter days.

Preparation time:
25 minutes
+ overnight soaking
Total cooking time:
2 hours
Serves 4–6

1/4 cup dried peas (blue boilers)
2 tablespoons pearl barley
6 (750 g) lamb neck chops/rosettes
1.5 litres water
1 leek, cut into 2 cm pieces
1 turnip, cut into 1 cm cubes
1 large carrot, cut into 1 cm cubes
1 stick celery, sliced
2 cups shredded cabbage
salt, pepper
1/4 cup chopped fresh parsley

1 Place dried peas in a bowl. Cover with warm water; stand uncovered overnight.

Rinse and drain well.
2 Place peas, barley, chops and water in large heavy-based pan; bring to boil. Remove froth from the top; add leek and turnip. Reduce heat to low, simmer covered for 1½ hours.
3 Add carrot and celery to pan. Simmer uncovered for a further 30 minutes.
4 Add cabbage, stir until just heated through and tender; season to taste. Stir in parsley just before serving.
Note: Blue boilers are whole dried peas.

After removing froth, add the leek and turnip to pan.

Add cabbage, stir until just heated through and tender.

Cock-a-leekie

From Edinburgh.

Preparation time:
20 minutes
Total cooking time:
1 hour 45 minutes
Serves 6–8

1.2 kg chicken	*1 small bunch*
2 large leeks, chopped	*parsley*
1.5 litres water	*2 teaspoons salt*
1 bay leaf	*1 teaspoon cracked*
1 teaspoon fresh	*black pepper*
thyme leaves	*12 pitted prunes*

1 Rinse chicken under water both inside and out; drain well, pat dry with paper towel. Trim off excess fat; cut chicken in half.

2 Place chicken, leeks, water, herbs and salt in large heavy-based pan. Bring slowly to the boil; reduce heat to low. Simmer uncovered 1½ hours, removing froth occasionally. Discard bay leaf and parsley.

3 Carefully remove chicken halves from the pan; cool slightly. Shred flesh coarsely, discarding the skin and bones.

4 Return chicken to pan with pepper and prunes; stir until just heated through.

Note: Raisins can be used instead of prunes.

After trimming excess fat from chicken, cut it in half.

When chicken is cooked, remove bay leaf and parsley and discard.

After removing chicken from pan and cooling, shred flesh coarsely.

Add prunes and stir until just heated through.

Stovies

Use any leftover meat.

Preparation time:
15 minutes
Total cooking time:
50 minutes
Serves 4–6

---

*45 g butter or
dripping/lard
2 large onions,
coarsely chopped
1 kg potatoes, thickly
sliced
1 teaspoon salt
1/4 teaspoon ground
black pepper*

*1 cup water
1 cup shredded
leftover cooked
lamb
1 tablespoon finely
chopped fresh
parsley*

---

1 Heat butter or lard in medium heavy-based pan; add onions. Cook over low heat 5 minutes or until lightly golden.
2 Add potatoes, salt and pepper; toss until well coated.
3 Pour water down side of pan; cover with tight-fitting lid. Simmer gently for 35 minutes, shaking pan occasionally to prevent potatoes sticking or burning.
4 Add meat and parsley to pan. Shake pan gently. Simmer covered for a further 10 minutes.

Note: The name "stovies" refers to being cooked on the stove. This dish can also be cooked successfully in a closed vessel in the oven. Any leftover meat of your choice can be used in this dish to replace the lamb.
It can also be made without using meat at all, and is then known as Potato Stovies. Any type of potatoes may be used, including new potatoes. The cooking time will vary according to the type of potatoes chosen for the dish. It is often served with glasses of ice-cold buttermilk.

Add coarsely chopped onions to heated butter or lard.

Toss sliced potatoes in pan until they are well coated.

Pour water down side of pan, cover and simmer gently.

Add meat and parsley to the pan and shake pan gently.

Rumbledethumps

Very economical.

Preparation time:
20 minutes
Total cooking time:
45 minutes
Serves 4–6

---

450 g potatoes, chopped coarsely	**250 g cabbage, finely shredded**
60 g butter	**salt, pepper to taste**
1 large onion, thinly sliced	**2/3 cup grated cheddar cheese**

---

1 Preheat oven to moderate 180°C. Brush 23 cm pie dish with oil. Place potatoes in pan; cover with cold water. Bring to boil; reduce heat, simmer, uncovered, 8 minutes or until just tender. Remove from heat, drain. Rinse under cold water, drain again.

2 Transfer potatoes to bowl; mash coarsely with a fork.

3 Heat butter in pan. Add onion, cook over low heat 10 minutes or until soft and golden. Add cabbage, stir 5 minutes. Add potatoes, salt and pepper. Remove from heat, stir in 2 tablespoons cheese.

4 Transfer to dish; sprinkle with the remaining cheese. Bake 20 minutes.

Rinse potatoes under cold water and drain again.

In a bowl, mash drained potatoes coarsely with a fork.

Add potatoes, salt and pepper to cabbage in pan.

Sprinkle remaining cheese over top of mixture before baking.

Coat each fillet of trout with oatmeal after brushing with milk.

Add spring onions and parsley to butter, juice and peppercorns. Mix well.

SEAFOOD, MEAT & POULTRY

The cookery of Scotland reflects local availability of produce from both sea and land. There is an abundance of fish, and mutton is the most comonly used meat.

Crumbed Trout with Parsley Butter

Preparation time:
35 minutes
Total cooking time:
4 minutes
Serves 6–8

---

2 (500 g) large trout fillets, skin removed
2 teaspoons milk
1/4 cup fine oatmeal
1/4 cup oil

PARSLEY BUTTER
60 g butter, softened

3 teaspoons lemon juice
1/4 teaspoon cracked black peppercorns
1 spring onion, finely chopped
1 tablespoon finely chopped fresh parsley

---

1 Cut each fillet evenly into four pieces. Brush one piece of trout at a time with milk, then coat with oatmeal.

Repeat process with remaining fillets, milk and oatmeal. Arrange coated trout on a tray, cover with plastic wrap and refrigerate for 20 minutes.

2 To make Parsley Butter: Place butter in small bowl; mash with a fork. Gradually mix in lemon juice and peppercorns. Add spring onion and parsley; mix well.

3 It can be served in dollops or formed into a log shape and cut into rounds.

4 Heat oil in medium non-stick frying pan; add trout pieces. Cook over medium heat 2 minutes each side or until lightly golden. Serve with the parsley butter.

Form parsley butter mixture into a log shape.

Cook trout over medium heat for 2 minutes each side until lightly golden.

Mussel Stew

Use very fresh mussels.

Preparation time:
20 minutes
Total cooking time:
18 minutes
Serves 4

---

24 mussels
2/3 cup dry white wine
45 g butter
1 large onion, finely
  chopped
2 tablespoons plain
  flour
1 cup milk

1/2 cup cream
salt, pepper
2 tablespoons finely
  chopped fresh
  parsley
2 tablespoons lemon
  juice

---

1 Scrub mussels under cold running water. Remove beards; rinse and drain well. At this stage, discard any mussels that are open.
2 Place mussels in large, heavy-based pan with wine. Cover with lid, shake/toss over high heat for 1 minute. Remove from heat, strain; reserve liquid.
3 Heat butter in same pan. Add onion, stir over low heat for 10 minutes or until soft and golden. Add flour to pan, stir over medium heat for 1 minute.
4 Add reserved wine gradually to pan, stir until onion mixture is almost smooth; bring to the boil. Gradually blend in the milk. Simmer sauce for 2 minutes without stirring. Stir cream, salt and pepper, parsley and juice into sauce. Stir until just heated through. Add mussels, toss to coat with sauce. Simmer uncovered 3 minutes.

HINT
Any mussels that do not open properly during cooking must be discarded. If you are collecting your own shellfish, be careful that the area is not contaminated. Check with the locals. Remove any grit from mussels with a brush.

After scrubbing mussels under cold running water, remove beards.

Remove from heat and strain mussels, reserving liquid.

Add flour to onions in pan, stir for 1 minute.

Stir cream, salt and pepper, parsley and lemon juice into sauce.

Finnan Haddie

Famous Scottish dish.

Preparation time:
12 minutes
Total cooking time:
20 minutes
Serves 4

---

1 large onion, thinly sliced
500 g smoked haddock
1²/₃ cups milk
¹/₂ teaspoon cracked black pepper

1¹/₂ teaspoons mustard powder
20 g butter, softened
2 teaspoons plain flour
1 spring onion, finely chopped

---

1 Place onion over base of large pan. Cut haddock into 2 cm-wide pieces. Arrange over onion.
2 Blend milk, pepper and mustard; pour over fish. Bring slowly to the boil. Reduce heat to low, simmer covered for 5 minutes. Uncover and simmer for a further 5 minutes.
3 Remove fish to serving dish; keep warm. Simmer mixture in pan further 5 minutes, stirring.
4 Combine butter and flour. Add to pan with spring onions. Stir over low heat until mixture boils and thickens slightly. Pour over fish and serve.

Cut the smoked haddock into 2 cm-wide pieces.

Pour milk, pepper and mustard mixture over the fish in pan.

Remove fish from pan with slotted spoon and place on serving dish.

Add butter and flour mixture, with spring onion, to pan.

Partan Flan (Crab Flan)

This dish may be served hot or cold.

Preparation time:
20 minutes
+ 20 minutes
standing
Total cooking time:
50 minutes
Makes 25 cm round

1½ cups plain flour
50 g butter
50 g lard
2 tablespoons iced water
2 x 170 g cans crab meat, squeezed dry
2 eggs, lightly beaten
1¼ cups cream
1 small onion, grated

2 tablespoons finely chopped fresh parsley
1 tablespoon lemon juice
½ teaspoon salt
pinch cayenne pepper
¼ teaspoon ground nutmeg

---

1 Brush a shallow 25 cm flan tin with melted butter. Place flour, butter and lard in food processor bowl. Using pulse action, process for 15 seconds or until mixture is fine and crumbly. Add water, process 5 seconds or until mixture comes together.

2 Turn onto a lightly floured surface; press into a flattish round. Roll out pastry between two sheets of greaseproof paper, large enough to cover base and side of prepared tin; trim edges. Prick pastry evenly with a fork. Store pastry-lined tin, covered with plastic wrap, in refrigerator for 20 minutes.

3 Preheat oven to moderate 180°C. Spread crab into uncooked pastry case. Place eggs, cream, onion, parsley, juice, salt and cayenne in a jug. Beat with a whisk until well combined.

4 Pour cream mixture over crab. Sprinkle with nutmeg; bake for 50 minutes or until golden and cooked through.

Process flour, butter and lard until the mixture is fine and crumbly.

Trim pastry edges from flan tin and prick pastry with a fork.

Whisk egg and cream mixture in a jug until well combined.

Pour cream mixture over the crab and sprinkle with nutmeg.

Tweed Kettle (Poached Salmon)

Preparation time:
  5 minutes
Total cooking time:
  13 minutes
Serves 4

¼ cup fresh parsley
1½ cups fish stock
½ teaspoon salt
½ teaspoon cracked
  black pepper
pinch ground nutmeg
½ cup dry white wine

2 spring onions,
  finely chopped
4 salmon steaks,
  tail end
2 tablespoons finely
  chopped fresh
  parsley

1 Finely chop fresh parsley.
2 Combine stock, salt, pepper, nutmeg, wine and spring onions in shallow medium pan. Bring ingredients in pan slowly to the boil; boil 1 minute.
3 Place salmon in stock in a single layer. Simmer, covered, for 10 minutes. Remove salmon to serving plates with a slotted spoon; keep warm.
4 Boil stock 1 minute further; add parsley. Spoon liquid over salmon, serve immediately.

Note: This dish is named after the famous Tweed River in which salmon abound.

Using a sharp-bladed knife, finely chop fresh parsley.

Combine stock, salt, pepper, nutmeg, wine and spring onions in pan.

Add salmon to stock in pan, placing in a single layer.

Add chopped parsley to liquid in pan. Spoon over salmon.

Hotch Potch (Lamb Stew)

Preparation time:
25 minutes
Total cooking time:
1 hour 45 minutes
Serves 4–6

---

1 tablespoon oil
3 lamb shanks
(1 kg)
1 large onion,
chopped
1 large turnip,
chopped
1 stick celery, chopped
1 litre water
2 teaspoons salt
1 teaspoon cracked
black pepper

300 g cauliflower,
chopped
2 carrots, chopped
1 cup frozen peas,
thawed
2 cups shredded
lettuce
2 tablespoons finely
chopped fresh
parsley

---

1 Heat oil in a large heavy-based pan; add lamb. Cook over medium heat for 10 minutes or until well browned all over. Add onion, turnip, celery, water, salt and pepper; bring to the boil. Reduce heat to low, simmer covered for 1 hour, stirring occasionally.

2 Add cauliflower, carrots and peas to pan. Simmer uncovered for 30 minutes.

3 Carefully transfer lamb from pan to chopping board with slotted spoon or tongs; cool slightly. Remove all flesh from bones and chop coarsely. Discard the bones.

4 Return lamb to pan with lettuce and parsley. Stir over low heat 3 minutes or until just heated through.

Note: Long, slow simmering of the lamb shanks in this recipe makes for extremely tender and sweet meat. It should be falling off the bones when ready to eat. It is a very economical dish.

Add onion, turnip, celery, water, salt and pepper to lamb.

Add cauliflower, carrots and peas to other ingredients in pan.

Carefully remove all flesh from bones, chop coarsely.

Return lamb to pan and add shredded lettuce and parsley.

Tuppeny Struggles (Mutton/Lamb Pies)

Preparation time:
25 minutes
Total cooking time:
1 hour 5 minutes
Makes 6

1 kg coarsely minced lamb
1 teaspoon salt
1/2 teaspoon ground black pepper
1 large onion, grated
3 spring onions, finely chopped
1 tablespoon worcestershire sauce
1/2 teaspoon ground nutmeg
1/2 cup rich beef stock
1/4 cup finely chopped fresh parsley
1/4 cup dried breadcrumbs
1 egg, lightly beaten

PASTRY
200 g lard/dripping
1 cup water
3 cups plain flour
1/2 teaspoon salt

1 Preheat oven to moderate 180°C. Brush six 2/3-cup capacity round, oval or square pie dishes with melted butter or oil. Place lamb, salt, pepper, onion, spring onions, sauce, nutmeg, stock, parsley and breadcrumbs into a large bowl. Mix with hand until ingredients are well combined.

2 To make Pastry: Place lard or dripping and water in small pan. Stir over low heat 5 minutes or until lard has melted; remove from heat. Sift flour and salt in large mixing bowl. Make a well in centre; add lard mixture. Using a flat-bladed knife, stir liquid into flour until all liquid is absorbed and a soft dough forms. Turn pastry onto lightly floured surface, knead for about 30 seconds.

3 Divide pastry into six equal portions. Roll out two-thirds of each portion large enough to cover base and side of each prepared pie dish. (Remaining one-third of each portion will be used for pie lid.) Divide lamb mixture evenly into six portions. Press one portion at a time into each pastry-lined pie dish.

4 Roll out remaining portions of dough large enough to cover pies. Brush filling and pastry edge with egg; top each pie with pastry lid. Brush each top with egg; trim edges. Make two slits into top of each pie with a sharp knife. Bake for 1 hour or until crisp and well browned.

Note: Once the pastry has been kneaded, work quickly to prevent it hardening and becoming difficult to work with.

Mix ingredients with hand until well combined.

Stir liquid into flour with flat-bladed knife.

Press one portion of lamb at a time into each pastry-lined pie dish.

After brushing top of pastry with egg, trim edges.

Scotch Collops in the Pan

Preparation time:
6 minutes
Total cooking time:
15 minutes
Serves 4

---

45 g butter
2 large onions
250 g mushrooms,
    sliced
4 thick scotch fillet
    steaks (800 g total)

2 tablespoons whisky
2 teaspoons plain
    flour
1/2 cup chicken stock
salt, pepper

---

1 Heat butter in large frying pan; add sliced onions. Cook over medium heat for 5 minutes; add mushrooms. Stir over medium-high heat for 5 minutes or until lightly golden. Push to one side of pan.
2 Add steaks to pan. Cook over medium-high heat 3 minutes each side.

3 Spread onions and mushrooms around meat; add whisky, shake pan. Transfer steaks to serving plate; keep warm.
4 Add flour to pan; stir over medium heat 1 minute. Add stock gradually. Stir for 2 minutes or until sauce boils and thickens. Season; spoon over steaks.

Add mushrooms to onions in pan; stir until lightly golden.

Add steaks and cook over medium heat 3 minutes each side.

Spread onions and mushrooms around meat; add whisky, shake pan.

Gradually add stock to pan and stir until sauce boils and thickens.

Stoved Chicken

Tender and tasty.

Preparation time:
15 minutes
Total cooking time:
2 hours 20 minutes
Serves 6

12 chicken pieces	**3 large onions, thinly**
salt, pepper	**sliced**
1 tablespoon oil	**3 cups rich chicken**
1.5 kg potatoes,	**stock**
thickly sliced	**60 g butter, melted**

1 Trim chicken pieces of excess fat; pat dry with paper towel. Rub with salt and pepper.
2 Heat oil in deep heavy-based saucepan. Add half the chicken pieces. Cook over medium heat about 8 minutes or until well browned. Remove; repeat with remaining pieces.
3 Arrange one-quarter potatoes over base of pan. Top with one-quarter of the onions and four pieces of chicken. Repeat layering process, ending with onions.
4 Pour chicken stock and butter over ingredients in pan. Cover with a sheet of greased greaseproof paper and the lid. Bring to the boil; reduce heat to low. Simmer 2 hours.

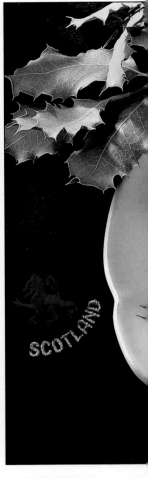

Rub trimmed chicken pieces with salt and pepper.

Cook chicken in oil until it is well-browned all over.

Place one-quarter of the onions over the potatoes.

Cover pan with a sheet of greased greaseproof paper.

Roastit Bubble-Jock (Christmas Turkey)

Preparation time:
  25 minutes
Total cooking time:
  2 hours 20 minutes
Serves 6

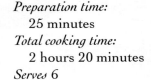

1/2 cup milk
1 1/4 cups coarse fresh breadcrumbs
1 stalk celery, finely chopped
1 small onion, finely chopped
1/3 cup chopped water chestnuts
300 g chicken livers, chopped
2 tablespoons finely chopped fresh parsley

pinch nutmeg
250 g sausage mince
1 teaspoon worcestershire sauce
3.4 kg self-basting turkey
2 cups warm water
60 g melted butter
2 tablespoons redcurrant jelly or plum conserve

1 Preheat oven to moderate 180°C. Combine milk, breadcrumbs, celery, onion, chestnuts, half the livers, one tablespoon parsley and nutmeg in a medium mixing bowl. Combine mince, remaining parsley and sauce in small bowl; mix well.
2 Rinse turkey thoroughly inside and out; wipe dry. Press breadcrumb mixture into turkey cavity. Seal end with skewers or string. Press the mince mixture into neck cavity; seal with either skewers or toothpicks. Place turkey on a rack in a deep baking dish. Add the water to the dish with the turkey neck and remaining livers.
3 Brush the turkey all over with butter. Bake for 2 hours 10 minutes basting the turkey with pan juices occasionally. Remove from oven; transfer turkey to serving plate. Stand, covered, 10 minutes.
4 Place pan juices with livers and jelly into small pan. Boil over high heat for 10 minutes or until mixture reduces by half and a thin glaze forms. Stir constantly. Pass sauce through a fine strainer and serve with the turkey.
Note: Traditionally the stuffing was made with oysters and chestnuts. This recipe uses water chestnuts instead (available in cans) which produces a lighter result. Self-basting turkey is very moist when cooked because of the marinade placed in it by the manufacturer. It is a special treat at Christmas time for all the family. Serve with baked vegetables.

Combine milk, breadcrumbs, celery, onion, chestnuts, half livers and parsley, nutmeg.

Press mince mixture into neck cavity. Seal ends.

Brush turkey all over with butter using a pastry brush.

Pass sauce through a fine strainer before serving with the turkey.

Stir oatmeal over low heat until lightly toasted.

Beat the cream in a small bowl until soft peaks form.

DESSERTS

The frugal, self-sufficient way of life that existed in the early days in Scotland and still exists in some parts today, is evident in these recipes.

Cranachan or Cream Crowdie

Strawberries may be substituted.

2 tablespoons medium oatmeal	**2 x 250 g punnets raspberries**
1 cup cream	**2 tablespoons rolled oats, toasted**
2 tablespoons honey	
1 tablespoon whisky	

Preparation time:
  12 minutes
  + 2 hours
    refrigeration
Total cooking time:
  5 minutes
Serves 6

1 Place oatmeal in small pan. Stir over low heat 5 minutes or until lightly toasted. Remove from heat; cool completely.
2 Using electric beaters, beat cream in small mixing bowl until soft peaks form. Add honey and whisky; beat until just combined.
3 Fold cooled, toasted oatmeal into the cream mixture using a metal spoon.
4 Begin layering the raspberries and cream evenly between six tall dessert glasses, ending with the cream. Refrigerate for 2 hours. Serve sprinkled with toasted oats.
Note: To toast oats, place on a small, shallow tray. Toast under a hot grill until lightly golden.
In Scotland, charms are placed into cranachan at Halloween, somewhat like the customary coins in English Christmas puddings.

Using a metal spoon, fold toasted oatmeal into cream mixture.

Layer raspberries and cream evenly between six tall dessert glasses.

Butterscotch Tart

A delicious special treat. May be served with whipped cream.

Preparation time:
20 minutes
+ 20 minutes
standing
Total cooking time:
1 hour 5 minutes
Makes 22 cm round

---

2 cups plain flour
125 g butter, chopped
2 tablespoons caster
  sugar
1 egg yolk
1 tablespoon iced
  water

FILLING
3/4 cup soft brown
  sugar

1/3 cup plain flour
1 cup milk
45 g butter
1 teaspoon vanilla
  essence
1 egg yolk

MERINGUE
2 egg whites
2 tablespoons caster
  sugar

---

1 Preheat oven to moderate 180°C. Brush a deep, 22 cm flan tin with melted butter. Sift flour into large bowl; add butter. Using fingertips, rub butter into flour 3 minutes or until mixture is fine and crumbly; stir in sugar. Add yolk and water, mix to soft dough; press into ball.
2 Roll pastry between two sheets of plastic wrap, to cover base and side of prepared tin; trim edges. Prick pastry evenly with a fork. Store pastry-lined tin, covered with plastic wrap, in refrigerator for 20 minutes. Cut a sheet of greaseproof paper large enough to cover pastry-lined tin. Spread layer of dried beans or rice evenly over paper. Bake 35 minutes, remove from oven; discard paper and beans/rice.

3 To make Filling: Place sugar and flour in small heavy-based pan. Make well in centre. Using a whisk, add milk gradually, stirring to a smooth paste. Add butter. Stir with whisk over low heat 8 minutes or until mixture boils and thickens. Remove from heat, add essence and yolk; whisk until smooth. Spread filling into precooked pastry case; smooth surface.
4 Place egg whites in small, dry bowl. Using electric beaters, beat egg whites until firm peaks form. Add sugar gradually, beating constantly until mixture is thick and glossy and all the sugar is dissolved. Spoon meringue over filling and swirl into peaks using a fork or flat-bladed knife. Bake 20 minutes or until meringue is lightly golden. Serve warm or cold.

Add yolk and water to butter and flour; mix to a soft dough.

Roll pastry between two sheets of plastic wrap to cover base and side of tin.

Add vanilla essence and egg yolk; whisk until smooth.

When egg whites form firm peaks, add sugar gradually, beating constantly.

Queen Mary's Tart

Serve with whipped cream.

Preparation time:
8 minutes
+ 20 minutes
refrigeration
Total cooking time:
45 minutes
Makes 22 cm round

---

250 g packet puff pastry	*4 eggs, lightly beaten*
2 tablespoons apricot jam	*1/2 cup dried mixed peel*
90 g butter	*1/4 cup sultanas*
1/3 cup caster sugar	*3 teaspoons self-raising flour, sifted*

1 Preheat oven to hot 240°C (200°C gas). Brush a deep 22 cm flan tin with melted butter.
2 Roll out pastry to line base and side of prepared tin; trim edges. Refrigerate 20 minutes. Prick pastry evenly with a fork; bake 10 minutes.

Remove from oven; spread base with jam.
3 Using electric beaters, beat butter and sugar in small mixing bowl until light and creamy. Add eggs gradually, beating thoroughly after each addition. (Mixture will appear curdled.) Add fruit and flour; beat on low speed 20 seconds or until just combined.
4 Pour mixture into cooled pastry case; bake 10 minutes. Reduce temperature to moderately hot 210°C (190°C gas), bake tart a further 25 minutes or until skewer comes out clean when inserted into filling. Serve warm or cold.
Note: It is important to pre-bake the pastry case for a crisp base. Pastry will shrink slightly during baking. This is a delicious light cake-like mixture in a pastry shell. It may be served with custard which has a little brandy stirred through.

Brush a deep 22 cm flan tin with melted butter.

After refrigerating pastry for 20 minutes, prick evenly with a fork.

Add fruit and flour to creamed mixture in bowl. Beat until combined.

Carefully pour mixture into the cooled pastry case.

Clootie Dumpling

Preparation time:
10 minutes
Total cooking time:
2½ hours
Serves 6–8

---

*3 cups self-raising
    flour
1 cup prepared/
    packaged suet mix
1 cup currants
½ cup sultanas
½ cup raisins,
    chopped
¾ cup caster sugar*

*1½ teaspoons ground
    cinnamon
1½ teaspoons mixed
    spice
½ teaspoon
    bicarbonate of soda
1 egg, lightly beaten
2 cups buttermilk*

---

1 Brush an 8-cup capacity pudding steamer with melted butter. Sift flour into large mixing bowl. Add suet mix, fruit, sugar, spices and soda. Stir with a wooden spoon. Make a well in centre; add egg and milk. Stir until all ingredients are well mixed; do not overbeat.

2 Spoon mixture into prepared steamer; smooth surface.

3 Cover with a pleated, greased sheet of foil, then a tight–fitting lid. Place in a large saucepan.

4 Pour in enough boiling water to come two-thirds up the side of the steamer. Cover with saucepan lid. Reduce heat to low, simmer covered for 2½ hours, topping up water level if necessary during cooking. Remove pudding from pan, turn onto serving plate. Serve warm or cold with custard or cream.

Note: In frugal households, these were made to help celebrate birthdays. Greaseproof paper was wrapped around threepenny pieces and these were added to the dumplings. Each family member hoped to get a coin.

Add suet mix, fruit, sugar, spices and soda to flour in bowl.

After spooning mixture into steamer, smooth the surface.

Cover steamer with pleated, greased sheet of foil.

Pour boiling water to come two-thirds up the side of the steamer.

BURNS' NIGHT FARE

Atholl Brose

Preparation time:
  5 minutes
  + 30 minutes
  standing
Total cooking time:
  nil
Makes 1 litre (4 cups)

> *3/4 cup fine oatmeal*
> *1 cup warm water*
> *2 teaspoons honey*
> *1/2 cup Drambuie*
> *1/2 cup thick*
>   *pure cream*

1 Place the oatmeal into a medium mixing bowl. Make a well in centre. Gradually add the water, stirring with a wooden spoon. Leave, covered, with a tea-towel, 30 minutes.
2 Pass oatmeal mixture through a coarse strainer into a clean jug, pressing until the oatmeal is dry; reserve liquid, discard oatmeal. Strain the liquid a second time, passing it through a fine strainer into a clean jug.
3 Add Drambuie, honey and cream. Whisk until well combined. Pour into sterilised jars or bottles. Shake well. Store, sealed, in a cool dark cupboard.
Note: Shake Atholl Brose before using.

Haggis

Preparation time:
  30 minutes
Total cooking time:
  4 hours
Serves 4–6

> *1 set sheep's heart,*
>   *lungs and liver*
> *2 medium onions,*
>   *finely chopped*
> *1 teaspoon salt*
> *1/2 teaspoon pepper*
> *1 teaspoon nutmeg*
> *1/2 teaspoon mace*
> *1 cup medium*
>   *ground oatmeal*
> *3 cups finely chopped*
>   *suet*
> *1 cup beef stock*
> *1 ox bung*

For Atholl Brose: Press oatmeal mixture through a coarse strainer into a jug.

Add Drambuie, honey and cream to jug. Whisk until well combined.

1 Trim meat of excess fat and sinew, discard windpipe if present. Place in a large pan, cover with water. Bring to the boil, reduce heat and simmer for 1 hour. Drain and cool.

2 Chop meat finely, Combine in a large bowl with onions, salt, pepper, nutmeg, mace, oatmeal, suet and stock; mix well.

3 Stuff meat mixture into ox bung. Divide in half and tie open ends securely with string. Leave enough room for mixture to expand otherwise it will burst whilst cooking. Place in pot. Cover with water. Bring to boil, reduce heat and simmer, covered, for 3 hours. Do not boil vigorously or haggis may burst. Serve hot, with mashed potatoes and turnips.

For Haggis: Add stock to meat, onions, salt, pepper, nutmeg, mace, oatmeal and suet.

Tie open ends of haggis securely with string, leaving enough room for expansion.

INDEX